Hello my name is Thomas and this is my second book focussing on my ongoing battle with depression following on from Sunshine and Darkness.

I still have my bad days and I still have my good days, the main thing that changed for me was recognising that the bad days do indeed pass, granted that some may last longer than others and sometimes I cannot find my way out of the maze that is depression.

I write about my experiences in the maze in poetic form and I will try and add a footnote about what I was feeling or thinking about at the time to give you a deeper understanding of my experience.

I am still new to talking about my experiences and at times my writing may appear raw and deep but I don't edit my pieces so what you're reading is exactly what I first wrote.

My ultimate goal with this book and its predecessor is to simply show you that you are not alone and even though I may not know exactly what you're going through, hopefully I can shine a little light for you to follow and find your way out of your own maze. I also want to break the stigma/taboo of talking about depression, no one should ever feel bad for expressing how they feel.

Anyway that's enough of my rambling, I hope the following pieces show you that you're not alone and there is always hope no matter how dark it seems.

Deep within
There lives a voice
So subtle and slight
But in that voice
This poet lives
And dies…

The Maze

Deep within the maze
I didn't bring matches
Was that a sound?
My breath catches
I hate this place
But yet it feels like home
Darkness envelops me
Leaving me all alone
Bringing comfort
And trepidation both
"Survive the night"
I repeatedly quoth
My eyes adjust slowly
And I spot a clearing
Here I shall await
As fear is slowly nearing
Threatening to consume
And devour my remains
I hopelessly beg
One day I'll break these chains...

This piece was the reason for this books title, follow me through the maze and out the other end.

That's how it goes

That's how the story goes
They all leave in the end
The timing may change
But promises always bend
Before they break completely
Shattering upon the floor
Leaving me here alone
Forevermore

That's how the story goes
They all let you down
Build you up high
Even place upon your head a crown
But that just intensifies the fall
The fall onto my knees
Leaving me broken and gasping
With unanswered pleas

That's how the story goes
That's how I turned cold
A cynical hermit
A recluse no longer bold
This heart is patched up
With bandages and tape
Locked under a stone exterior
Away from anyone to rape…

I have had a lot of people walk into my life and quickly run back out but I have to
remind myself two things.
1, People always come into our lives to teach us something.
2, The right people do indeed stay.

I've not treated you right

I've not treated you right
I wish I had foresight
That every insult
Hit like a bolt
I'm sorry for who I am
I never really gave a damn

I've not treated you right
Now these claims have come to light
I abused, debased and belittled
Against your confidence I whittled
I'm sorry for not growing
For no love showing

I've not treated you right
I was worse at night
Away from watching eyes
I broke you with lies
I called you worthless and stupid
A constant voice you couldn't rid

I've not treated you right
I tried as hard as I might
To change for the better
To keep my word to the letter
But this time will be different I swear
Oh mirror on the wall I swear...

Self love was one of the hardest I ever had to learn and I'd be lying if I said I had
this mastered yet, I still don't recognise who I see in the mirror but every day I see
myself a little better.

I'm coming home

I'm coming home
I'm feeling okay today
I'm being released
From this padded cell
That cushioned my fall from grace

I'm coming home
I'm sorry for the pain
The hurt, anguish and shame
I'm sorry I failed the family
But today I'm smiling

I'm coming home
Please don't make a fuss
Or come and meet me off the bus
It's not a special moment
Except to me

I'm coming home
Maybe it was too soon
I find too much solace in the moon
Maybe I'm just a lunatic
And my home isn't really here with you…

Where do you go when home isn't home anymore? if you find the answer to this
then please let me know as I still haven't found this out.

My Compass

Walks along the beach
Dipping toes in the sea
You'll look at me and smile
I've never been this happy
Fingers interlocked
Like the zip on my hoodie you stole
Too be fair it looks better on you
And you make my world whole
Your smile and eyes
Tell me I've found the one
Somebody call off the search
It's finally done
The sun kisses your cheeks
And a million freckles appear
My past may have been stormy
But my future looks so clear
For even if we hit rough seas
We'll navigate through
Because you're my compass
Keeping me true…

I've been very lucky, after abusive relationships, to find a partner who accepts my dark days and sometimes sits with me in the maze, she honestly is my compass and occasionally, I write her little pieces like this to show her how much she means to me.

Hello

Hello pain
My old friend
Thank you for dropping in
I'm no longer asleep
Woken from my eternal slumber

Hello grief
My old confidant
Thank you for stopping by
To let fall again
I got too high without you

Hello depression
It's been awhile
Thank you for making an appointment
Although did you ever truly leave
Or was it a sunny day

Hello heartache
My old partner
Thank you for the proof
That my heart isn't diamond
More diamond plated

Hello sorrow
Glad you took a moment
To get to know me again
I guess you have never been far
No matter how much the clock turns...

Self love is so important in this battle and i've always likened depression to a wave,
until you learn how to surf, you'll keep falling under and not riding it like you should.
I'm still consumed by the wave at times but my surfing skills are improving.

My Demons

My demons
They shout at me
Tell me I'm useless
Put me down with insults
Then bring me back with a compliment
And still I listen

My demons
They belittle me
Make me feel 5 foot tall
Have me believe I'm still a boy
Whilst telling me I'm handsome
And still I listen

My demons
They make me drink
Cry and plead all night
Make me whisper under my breath
But in day time they disappear
And still I listen

My demons
They make me cut
To bleed for them
To feel the pain they want
But then tell me I'm brave
And still I listen

I've had these demons
For years it seems
And they try to kill me nightly
But whilst I know they lie
Still I listen...

What can I say here that I haven't already?

Help me?

People walk past
Barely looking at me
I'm sure they heard me
Maybe I whispered
"Help me please"

I'm no vagabond
No beggar or ruffian
I'm just in need of an ear
Someone to listen
"Help me please"

I'm not looking for money
No quick coin or buck
I'm only looking for humanity
To be more than a burden
"Help me please"

I don't drink
Smoke or take drugs
Unless you count coffee
But what I'm after I cannot buy
"Help me please"...

It took years of asking the wrong people for help until I found the right outlet, I now have the help I need, help is out there if you are ready and if you're not then that's okay as well.

Mind and body

I'm a tourist
Sight seeing
Taking photos
Of a by gone age
A land that time forgot

I'm an intruder
I don't belong here
Everything is alien
Everything is just off
And altogether wrong

I'm a wanderer
Roaming this world
Trying to find references
A point of interest
But alas I'm all at sea

I'm a nomad
I belong to no home
No place is mine
How long can I live as a stranger
In my own mind and body?

If only I could reach the nirvana of having mind and body aligned, I have tried yoga
and pilates but felt stupid and meditation really wasn't for me but I find a strange
zen like existence when writing, just proving that peace can come in many forms.

Don't Play

Don't play with me
My heart isn't as strong as before
The last player didn't press reset
They left me on continue
But with no intention to insert more coins
So here I stand
Solitary and weary
My casing looks solid
But my wiring is shot
Just look a little closer
So please don't play with me
Unless you can defeat
My final boss…

Far too often I wear my heart on my sleeve, I tell everyone openly about my problems and this has left me vulnerable and abused in the past, so now I ask people not to play with me until they know what they're playing with.

I cannot carry on

I cannot carry on
I'm a burden
I'm a disappointment
I'm just not good enough
So off I go
Into the sunset

I cannot carry on
I failed
I broke
Life's test was too much
So no goodbyes
As into the sunset I drift

I cannot carry on
I'm miserable
I'm depressed
No smile escapes
These lifeless lips
So with the sunset I'm gone

I cannot carry on
I asked for help
I begged for a lifeline
But I was greeted with silence
I was shunned
So off I went into the sunset…

This was written after a particularly bad night where I almost did something stupid to myself but instead I posted this on instagram and someone reached out to me which honestly saved my life.

I'm worth more

I'm worth more
Than missed messages
And waiting on hold
Waiting for you to decide
If I'm enough

I'm worth more
Than crossed wires
And mixed signals
You either want me
Or you want my attention

I'm worth more
Than lonely nights
And tears upon my pillow
As I lay wondering
If you're doing the same

I'm worth more
And more I will have
I will have happiness
Love and safety
No longer seemingly on the toss of a coin…

It took me the longest time to realise that I am indeed worth more than all of this
and so are you.

Trapped

You keep me alive
With a fire burning bright
You keep me moving forwards
Except at night
When the sun dips
And moon comes out
The voices inside my head
Begin to shout
They overpower me
They break me down
They belittle and degrade
Trapped inside my own town
I'm shouted at
I'm heckled and taunted
All inside this broken head
I'm sure I'm just haunted
I'm cursed and shunned
Left to wander till dawn
Then the light returns
And I'm reborn
Making the most of the sun's escape
Because when she dips below
These voices that lay dormant
In strength grow…

Why is it at night that demons come out to play? Is there a way to fully submerge
them? If there is then I haven't found it yet but I am hopefully I will find out one day.
Keep looking my friend.

Still

I've still got
Scars on my back
From your knife
A physical attack
It left me marked
A story I want to forget
But it surfaces
With every new threat

I've still got
Scars in my mind
From every insult
Each verbally unkind
I carry them with me
No matter the drug
Or therapy session
I cannot fully debug

I've still got
The same hang hate
For the body
You once called great
Just to turn on me
With razor bladed lyrics
Each barb cutting me down
Becoming my new critics...

How long must we carry former scars? Are mental scars similar to physical ones in
that we always carry them with us? Even when wrinkles form around them?

See it for yourself

I see it
In your eyes
You cried today
And that's okay
We all cry sometimes

I see it
In your body
You've broken
Against chains holding
You down to the ground

I see it
In your smile
You tried today
Gave it your best shot
And life discarded you

I see it
But maybe you don't
Not yet anyway
You're amazing
Now repeat this

I see it
I've cried
I've broken
I've tried
I'm doing amazing…

Try to remember that it's okay not to be okay, we all cry, we all break, we all try and
WE ARE ALL AMAZING, we are one tribe and in our tribe, no-one is left behind.

Time heals

Time heals they say
I hear it so often I began to believe
But time heals nothing
We just have to grieve

Time heals they say
Like an automated reply
If time does heal
Tell the clock I don't want to cry

Time heals they say
Patience and trust the path
Keep on track and you'll be fine
You having a laugh?

Time heals they say
By those who preach
Those who had a blessed life
Sunning themselves on a beach

Time heals they say
Well that's bull
Because no matter how much passes
Still I fall…

I really hate how taboo grief, loss and depression still is in society but what I hate
even more than that is the lazy sayings we have like: "Cheer up it might never
happen" or "Time heals all", if I had a pound for every time I heard this and more,
I'd be able to buy my own island by now.
Can we just normalise talking about things please?

I remember the day

I remember the day
When time stood still
I couldn't make it move
With no amount of will

I remember the day
My world turned upside down
When I felt so alone
In this big old town

I remember the day
When you came and spoke
At that very moment
My heart broke

I remember the day
I never got to say goodbye
I remember that day clearly
As every day since, I cry...

I still remember the gut wrenching anguish and also remember how numb I felt with
every time death has visited my life, casually walking in, taking some-one and then
walking back out without rhyme or reason.

I did what I did

I did what I did
To survive
At the detriment to none
But myself
I cut
I bruised
I did what I did
To survive

I did what I did
To breathe
I peeled back my ribs
And opened my soul
I laid panting
Exhausted and in pain
I did what I did
To breathe

I did what I did
To love
To show compassion
And empathy to all
Except myself
I thought loving others
Would save me
I did what I did…

Repeat after me, self abuse is still abuse, I won't say stop it because that would
make me a hypocrite and I truly would hate to be called that.
Find a coping mechanism that isn't detrimental to your self or health, please.
As some-one who has woken up in hospital after drinking too much and blacking
out, as some-one who has cut himself repeatedly over the years and as some-one
who has sat on a bridge, dangled his legs over the edge and even kicked his shoes
into the river below, please find a better coping mechanism. Please.

Exposed emotions

Exposed emotions
Expose me
Time and time again
Damn this sleeve of mine

Exposed emotions
Explode from my lips
Curses and filth
Shock bystanders

Exposed emotions
Spewing unrelenting
Tears form
But only in my eyes

Exposed emotions
Betray what has happened
For I'm built like a wardrobe
And you're a bedside cabinet

Exposed emotions
Exposed lies
Exposed frailties
Exposed me.

Will I one day see men being able to talk about abuse freely? Without further abuse or ridicule? I remember from a past relationship where she screamed at me in the middle of the street for having a drink with friends and two happened to be women, the words she used still strike me, I remember that same day, I punched a wall and split my hand open as she made me angry and a police officer walked past and instantly placed himself between us, his back facing me and asking her if she wanted him to arrest me? A doorman came over and explained everything and only then did he accept I wasn't in the wrong and let me go.

The voice of the shadow

The voice of the shadow
Lives deep within me
It whispers and schemes
To send me off track
And ultimately
To my ruin
Far below
Away from salvation

The voice of the shadow
Has never been a friend
Although it seemed that way before
It drew me in
Made me think it was friendly
But as my old man always said
Beware my son
Because even wolves wear wool

The voice of the shadow
Has upped it's game lately
It feeds me falsehoods
And weaves lies
I cannot see the end game
But as tears stream in my eyes
I figure it out all too late
As the pills are now gone...

The glamour of silence

The glamour of silence
Feels the air
Birds didn't get the memo
But that's okay
The little squeaks send me away
Into a deep slumber
Off to a far away land
Filled with memories of things yet to come

The glamour of silence
Floods my ears
The absolute stillness
Of the river and trees
All lazily flowing
In the slightest of breezes
And again I'm away
On a floating cloud

The glamour of silence
Is such a rarity
That sightings of unicorns
Are more familiar
In a world turned up to eleven
Silence is a virtue
Tell me this
When did you last hear silence?

As some-one who is battling depression, loss and ADHD, silence is truly a virtue, It
happens so rarely to me that I almost miss it when it happens.
When did you last hear silence? Have a think about that.

Let me sit and talk

Let me sit and talk
About a time not long ago
I hit rock bottom
And still I fell further
Into the abyss
Through the crack
And into the void
Never stopping

Let me sit and talk
About the free fall
I found my life in
I was lost
Alone and honestly scared
Two bottles spoke to me
So with both contents now gone
I slept an endless slumber

Let me sit and talk
About how I lost it all
I drowned without water
Went missing in a crowd
I screamed silently
And wept without tears
Please
Let me sit and just talk…

If I spoke, would you listen? Would you want to hear my story? Would you then tell
me yours?

Today

Today I lied
I actually cried
I sat in the shower
Going on a hour
With nowhere to hide

Today I blacked out
My demons ran about
They teased and run amuck
They never give a fuck
As in my head they shout

Today I drowned
I lost my ground
My footing slipped
My head dipped
And they pushed me down

Today is my last
I cannot outrun my past
It always catches me
I cannot be free
And so I live as an outcast…

I stumble a lot if I can be brutally honest, I spend days in bed, I cut off so many
people and I gave up on society some time ago, I constantly feel I don't have a
place anymore.

I deserve better

I deserve better
Better than double blue ticks
And messages left on read
Voicemail conversations
And unanswered hellos

I deserve much better
Than fleeting glances
And slight touches
Kisses on the cheek
And smiles unanswered

I deserve so much better
Than an empty bed
Except when you have an itch
I have to scratch
And then with dawn you're gone

I demand better
Than being an option
A play thing to use
Than discard
I deserve better…

We all deserve better than this, You are deserving of love, attention and happiness.
Too often we settle for less because we cannot see further along.

Slipping away

I feel it ebbing away
My sanity waning
My mask has broken
This facade isn't worth maintaining
I need help
Or maybe I'm already crazy
And should finally give in
And accept pills to make me hazy

A padded cell with no windows
And a jacket to match
Secured safe and sound
With a door without a latch
Throw me in
Melt the key
I'll just have these voices
As my company...

I wrote this on a particularly bad day, not bad in any normal way but after a day of forcing myself to socialise with too many people, i didn't look after my battery very well and this came out.

Changed

I feel myself
Slowly slipping
My confidence waning
My smile dipping
Laughs are few and far
Even my eyes don't shine
I'm no longer okay
I'm no longer fine

I feel myself
Well no I don't anymore
I no longer sleep
My feet drag upon the floor
I'm different now
I'm not the same
I don't even know
If I can keep my name

I've changed
As a whole
I have no purpose
No final goal
Just living day to day
Sunrise to sunset
Drinking away my nights
Hoping to forget…

I'm trying to remind myself that change is a part of life and I'm not the same person
I was twenty years ago or even ten years ago and that's okay.
We shouldn't ever feel bad for changing and I mean ever.

Road

I walk alone
Down this road
Demons heckle
Monsters goad
They try to divert
Me from this path
Away from my smile
And innocent laugh

They offer insults
Drugs and drinks
Affairs of the heart
And other kinks
But on the road I remain
Stoic and resolute
For I've fallen off before
And it's anything but cute…

Our own demons can honestly destroy us if we let them.
Being alone isn't always the answer but until I love myself, I cannot let anyone else in.

Finally free

Chains tied to my legs
Drags me into the deeps
And into my pores
Depression creeps
Further I fall
Unable to swim
The current is too strong
My hopes seem slim

Finally my ties undone
I can kick free
My head is above water
I can now see
Swimming for the shore
I'm tired and worn
But now I know
A new person is born…

Depression, for me at least, is a wave but sometimes I suck at surfboarding.
I try to ride this wave and sometimes I succeed and others, well, I fall on my face.
Both are completely fine and I'm trying to remember that.

Poet born

I was created
In a wild storm
Blue eyes so deep
And poet born
I was created
And brought into life
To lead the way
And clear strife

I was created
To shine a light
To drive away darkness
And always fight
I was created
To be a voice
I may have been created
But existing is my choice…

Just a little glimpse into who I am.
I will always offer life jackets to those who are drowning.
I will always listen to those who have so much to say.
I will always speak for those with no voice.
I will always leave a light on for those who are lost.

Pain

Pain tears through me
Ripping my soul asunder
Untying my life strings
Leaving me motionless
Breathless upon the floor

Pain tears through me
A life changing event
A world ended
In one fateful year
I am undone

Pain tears through me
As tears flow freely
Leaving my body
Like a rental agreement
Coming to an end

Pain tears through me
As I remodel myself
My pen as my guide
A tribe backing me
As this pain is repurposed...

I write through tears and pain and also lay in bed with tears and pain, sometimes I win, sometimes I lose.

My Bed

My bed has turned cold
Like my heart
It's filled with sex
But not love
Passion but no warmth

My bed has become big
Since you left it
I surprisingly take up little space
You hogged the quilt after all
But now it envelops me

My bed has become a table
A sofa and den
Because on some days
It becomes my refuge
My safe place in a world of hurt

My bed has become worn out
But I cannot replace it
Because if I do
Then what would be left
Of us, Of me…

What can I say? My bed had so many uses in the past, now it is used just for laying
awake and wondering what if?

Standing all alone

I'm standing all alone
In a field of barley and oat
My head barely rises above
Almost as if afloat
On a golden sea
Hoping for a tide to flow
And take me far away
Away from this golden glow

I'm standing all alone
Upon desert sands
Carried on a wind so strong
I cannot lift my hands
Wind and sand batters
Blasting away this fake shell
Exposing my soul to the world
With no voice left to yell

I'm standing all alone
Barely atop an ice sheet
My body turns blue
I cannot feel my feet
My legs won't move
I cannot escape or fall
Maybe the sunshine
Wasn't so bad after all

I'm awake in my bed
The sun hasn't rose yet
I quickly wrote this down
As to not forget
Every place and time
Is a blessing in any guise
And with a satisfied smile
I rolled over and closed my eyes…

I've not treated you right

I've not treated you right
I wish I had foresight
That every insult
Hit like a bolt
I'm sorry for who I am
I never really gave a damn

I've not treated you right
Now these claims have come to light
I abused, debased and belittled
Against your confidence I whittled
I'm sorry for not growing
For no love showing

I've not treated you right
I was worse at night
Away from watching eyes
I broke you with lies
I called you worthless and stupid
A constant voice you couldn't rid

I've not treated you right
I tried as hard as I might
To change for the better
To keep my word to the letter
But this time will be different I swear
Oh mirror on the wall I swear…

I still, to this day, fail to treat myself right, I am trying and I'm learning that trying is a
good place to start.

Quiet Rebellion

Quiet rebellion
Slowly builds
As each verbal attack
Builds my defences
I won't strike back though
No verbalisation from my lips
No venom shall pass my teeth
It's not in my vocabulary
Even though you're fluent in speech
And strike deep into my soul

Quiet rebellion
Has brewed a long time
Like the way one brews a tea
Before enjoying the beverage
Today is the day
The rebellion comes to a head
When you come home
My stuff will be gone
I'll be forgotten in time
But this rebellion will stay true…

My biggest and perhaps over reaching aim in life is simple really, I want to inspire other people, no matter of race, creed, sex or religion, to be free to talk about what torments them, no matter how small it seems to be. I want to create a safe space for no problem to be belittled or disregarded.

Perhaps I'm a dreamer but I hope I'm not the only one.

Suffocating the senses

Suffocating the senses
My anxiety rips me apart
Leaving me standing motionless
Except for the shivers
That run down my spine
Leaving goosebumps along the way

Suffocating the senses
My confidence depletes
Over thinking has won this time
Second, third, fourth guessing
Should I just give up
And give in to these thoughts

Suffocating the senses
My eyes water
My sight goes blurry
As a storm floods over me
Leaving me barely treading water
Soon to drown

Suffocating the senses
A bottle is opened
The sweet cool nectar
Flows so smoothly down my throat
All cares forgotten
As my demons and I drink…

Being a writer and poet I feel a lot, I'm usually overwhelmed and it took me the longest time to learn that this is okay.
I barely drink anymore to drown my demons and that's a good start at least, I do still shout back at them from time to time but I'm learning to live with them and not let them define who I am or who I want to be.

The cracks

Fall in love with the cracks
The imperfections I hold
Within my broken soul
And withered heart
My defences are worn
My attack is weak
I've built myself up
On top of a ruined temple
Longing to be loved again
To feel the warmth of a touch
So please I beg
Fall in love with the cracks
For they are me
And I am them…

I am my flaws, my flaws are me.
I am still human, I am still good.
I am still learning, I am still incomplete.
I am enough. I AM ENOUGH.

Beauty

There's beauty in the broken
In the damned
In the darkest corners of a society
That has discarded us from use
Because we didn't fit in

There's beauty in the broken
Those who cry every night
The ones who sit in the glow of the moon
Wondering what could've been
Or what is yet to come

There's beauty in the broken
Just be careful with jagged edges
They may still be sharp
But they aren't meant to harm
They're just our last defence

There's beauty in the broken
I've seen it first hand
It makes me remember
Some words my old man once said
Broken crayons still colour the same…

For the longest time I considered myself broken and took it as an absolute, broken is all I was and all I could be.

I was wrong, I now call myself healing and not broken but I do like the idea of owning the broken tag and turning it into a positive.
Something like "Yes I've hit rock bottom, Yes I broke but I'm still here, I'm still fighting"
What do you think?

An ode to winter porridge

I walk in
Table for one please
It's freezing outside
I'd like a coffee and porridge
The coffee warms my hands
The porridge though
Warms my soul
A perfect blend of spices
A temperature just right
Blueberries scattered on top
Oh this porridge right here
Is what the bears were searching for
Thankfully we have no bears anymore
As I'm not sharing this
Even goldilocks
Would have trouble
Separating me from this bowl
This bowl of pure winter heaven…

This is my favourite winter time memory and who doesn't love porridge right? I am part bear and part Scottish after all.
Not a piece about mental health exactly but in a way it is, over the winter lockdown we had here, my favourite restaurant closed and with it, took away this beautiful breakfast.
It is the most important meal of the day after all.

Doesn't work

These tablets don't work anymore
They no longer help me sleep
They lock me in a comatose state
Unable to move or feel
But thoughts still run free

These drinks don't work anymore
I no longer get drunk
The once sweet nectar
Has all of a sudden turned bitter
And into a symbiotic relationship

Sex doesn't work anymore
The once skyscraper high
Has now hit a chasm low
And all I'm left with
Is notches on a worn out bed post

This writing doesn't work anymore
It's no longer cathartic
In fact it's slowly killing me
Drowning me from the inside
Without a life raft in sight…

One morning I woke up to find all of my coping mechanisms ceased to work, I then heard an interview with Jim Carrey in which he described being depressed as needing deep rest, it honestly struck a nerve with me as I had never thought of depression in that way before. He explained that it the souls way of saying it needs deep rest from the character you currently play.
I don't know if he was right or wrong but I took that deep rest, quit all toxicity in my life and almost started from scratch, it seemed to help, at least a little bit.

Nothing special

I'm nothing special
A nomad of sorts
Looking for my forever home
A place to rest my hat
Until then I'll be gone

I'm nothing special
A passing moment
A fleeting embrace
The quickest of kisses
And then gone again

I'm nothing special
I won't be remembered
I might cross your mind one day
But when you look for me
I'll be gone again

I'm nothing special
A speck of star dust
In a universe infinite
On a crowded rock I stay
Gone invisible again…

I remember writing this and at the time I genuinely thought I was nothing special, then a message from a close friend on instagram proved me wrong, they had really dark thoughts and was in a very dark place when they read through my poems, I won't go into details out of pure respect but they saw through my words that they wasn't alone.
Needless to say but I broke down into tears and almost jumped a plane to the states just to be there for them.
No matter how dim, keep your light shining, you never know who is watching.

When I leave

When I leave
Did I go in debt?
Unpaid dues and bills
Did I forget?
If so I'm sorry
To whom pays my arrears
It wasn't my plan
To leave you in tears
It was my time
The hourglass emptied
All I owed I promise
Wasn't built from greed
May you forgive
Anything left to pay
I didn't mean it
As my name begins to decay

When I leave
May I go in credit
Whom people quoth
My final writ
I hope I built foundations
I hope I did good
I pray I helped people
From under my depressive hood
May my name live on
Being a light to those
Whoever out there
That depression chose
I want you to break those chains
And live your best life
And place upon me
All leftover strife…

There

There's a house
That's missing someone special
Someone's smile
And warm heart
I wish you was in it

There's a bench
By the riverside
Birds waddle by
Hoping I'd throw some food
I wish you was on it

There's a song
It plays late at night
They sing about a love so pure
So strong and everlasting
I wish you knew it

There's a dream I have
About warm cosy nights
Snuggled by the fire
No company except us
I used to wish you'd be in it...

I have love and lost but I still don't know if it is indeed better to have loved and lost
or never have loved at all.

I walk tall

I walk tall
Like a godlike being
Like a stoic warrior of old
Swinging a mighty axe with a shield
Felling the beast of lore

I walk tall
Like a viking from mythology
Drinking hard and fucking
Pillaging and raiding from sunrise to dusk
Carrying my tribe to victory

I walk tall
Like a Lord Knight of tales long gone
My armour cracked but holding
My blade slick with crimson life
And my heart unwavering

I walk tall
But I'll tell you a secret
It wasn't always so
I've cried in the shower at 3am
But simply no more tears fall…

I wrote this because of my love for warriors of old, did they carry the same burdens
that I do or are my problems tiny in comparison?

When I'm with you

When I'm with you
I feel at peace
I'm free to be myself
Be weird and loved
And never be scared

When I'm with you
I feel warmth
My soul ignites
My heart heals
And I'm whole

When I'm with you
I'm who I am
Not faking
Or hiding behind shades
I'm just me

When I'm with you
Light shines through
Breaking through my dark abyss
Showing me better days exist
With you I'm home…

I hate that I'm not my own saviour sometimes but feel lucky to have a supportive
tribe around me, they accept my flaws, my darkness and my bad days and they
never judge.

Decline

I'm in decline
Sliding down fast
Past rock bottom
And still I slide
Further

I'm in decline
Deteriorating quickly
My minds capacity
Has neared completion
No upgrades can be bought

I'm in decline
I barely eat as before
Or leave the house
Save for work that is
And so the decline deepens

I'm in decline
I'm forgetting who I am
Or who I was
Is there a factory reset button
Where I can tread a different path?

No longer declining
I'm at the end
I'm completely spent
My last memory wiped
No more tomorrows…

I wasn't in a good place when I wrote this, can you tell?
It took me the longest time to share these particular pieces with the world.

Standing in the rain

Standing in the rain
My head clears
The fog is lifted
And I see a new path
Laid out before me

Standing in the rain
It washes over me
Washing away these bad thoughts
Washing them down the drain
So I can stand again

Standing in the rain
I feel no cold
No numbness
No shiver escapes my lips
But a thank you does

Standing in the rain
I feel at peace
I feel cleansed
I feel reborn
I feel anew…

I don't know why and perhaps never will but I truly love standing in the rain, not a
little drizzle but a complete, skin soaking downpour.
For me, there is nothing better.

Invisible issues

Mental health issues
Are invisible till they're not
We think we're alone
Inside a box locked
Trapped with no way out
No matter how many people try

Depression is invisible
Until it's not
Trapped in a maze
Filled with haze
Completely blocked
Inside this labyrinth

Self harm is invisible
Until it's not
Claret flowing freely
To the bone nearly
As we choke
And tears flow

Crying is invisible
Until it's not
Breaking down at a bus stop
Or coffee shop
As people stop and stare
When all we want is someone to care...

I remember my first public breakdown, I was in a card shop buying a fathers day card for my dad like most of us do, except I got all the way to the till before remembering that he passed away two years prior, I completely broke down and ran out of the shop, I've never felt so embarrassed. It took me years to accept that I had nothing to be embarrassed about.

I spilt ink

I spilt ink
All over a page
I blotted and smudged
Whilst in a rage
And now a poem is made

I spilt ink
All over my skin
It made a river
Leaving a shiver
As down my arm it slithers

I spilt ink
Down my leg
An unseen tide
That I choose to hide
In shorts I have to resize

I spilt ink
In so many ways
Yet nobody knows
As the ink never shows
Blood as ink flows…

I am about to say two things here:

1, I self harmed a lot and not all in my younger days, some more recent.
2, I am 4 years without a single cut to my body.

I still remember

I still remember
The look on your faces
As I dressed you for school
And the tantrums that followed

I still remember
The excitement when you came home
Crashing through the door
To tell me about school

I still remember
Fish fingers and chips
Your favourite meal
When you came home with certificates

I still remember
Bed time book reading
Lord of the rings bookmarked
Sleepy eyes saying daddy please one more page

I still remember
Your laughs and giggles
Although day by day
They fade…

I cannot say anything else to this, even after all this time.

Demons

My legion of demons
Keep me under bended knee
They tell me I'm not enough
I'll never succeed

My legion of demons
Laugh at me
Calling me names
Pushing me into the mud

My legion of demons
Scoff when I fight
Swinging punches
Which they dodge easily

My legion of monsters
Expose my weaknesses
Play on my insecurities
And keep me cowed

My legion of demons
Feed off my self doubt
With a ravenous appetite
Time for a hunger strike…

My legion of demons still exist but i'm glad to say that the days and nights when
they over power me are getting less and less.

Frighten

Did it frighten you?
My brutal honesty
My truth regarding mental health
My blood soaked pages

Did it frighten you?
My dark abyss
That dwells deep within
This tortured soul

Did it frighten you?
My scars
How a blade met my skin
And I longed for the pain

Did it frighten you?
How I spoke of death
Of heartbreak and grief
With such candidness

Or did it frighten you
How I sat there smiling
Though tears escaped my eyes
And my soul ruptured…

I've always been someone who has kept his heart of his sleeve, for better or worse,
at least I can say I was always honest.
Hopefully one day mental health talks won't be taboo.

I feel it

I feel it infecting
Growing deep inside
Like a growl from inside a cave
It's head slowly waking

I feel it spreading
Through my veins
Spreading chaotic thoughts
Creating havoc within

I feel it intoxicating
Altering my genes
Terraforming my blood
Changing me fully from inside

I feel it overpowering
Like how a marionettes
Makes a puppet dance
To It's fateful tune

I feel it celebrating
Like how this final battle won the war
So now I surrender
My battle with mental health…

Do you ever feel depression rising but there is nothing you can do about it?
Welcome to my life.

Do you love me?

Do you love me enough
To let me go
To let me slip through your fingers
And drift off into the night

Do you love me enough
To fill this void within
Fill it with warmth
And make my heart beat once more

Do you love me enough
To allow me to be me
To not change me
But rather, let me grow with you

Do you love me enough
To help me stand on my own
To take fresh steps into this world
Off into the unknown

Do you love me enough
To make me believe in that four letter word
Or better yet shall I ask
Do you love me at all?

Is love meant to see all your flaws and love you more?
Is love meant to try and put your puzzle pieces back together?
Is love just a lie we tell each other to make us feel better?

Let me go

If you love me let me go
For I'm not meant for this life
I am an old soul
Born out of time

If you love me let me go
Back to days of old
Where morals and ethics align
And fantasy tales are told

If you love me let me go
I'm lost in this sea of technology
In these fleeting moments
That pass too quickly for me to hold

If you love me let me go
Let me find my way back
Back to a simpler age
Where words truly mattered

If you love me let me go
Please I'm dying here
A man out of time
And out of place I fear…

I'll repeat what I said just before, is love real or just a convenient lie we tell each other?

Slow train

The thing I love
About the slow train
Is all the fields
That scream past
The barns in glory
Some in disrepair
Sheep flocked together
A community of sorts
The horses more aloof
Like seven foot cats

The thing I love
About the slow train
Is how the landscape
Lazily sleeps on the horizon
Trees on their backs
Grass a form of blanket
The landscape looks peaceful
A Buddhist like hill

The thing I love
About the slow train
Is that time stills
Haste has no currency here
We all have to take a moment
And listen to the click clack of the rail
Maybe we have a nap
Maybe we get work done
Or maybe like me
We simply relax...

I really love the slow train.

Musical influences

Boys don't cry
I guess you're the Cure
I love a Waterloo sunset
You know my Kinks
I found somebody to love
You're my Queen
This is about a girl
You're my Nirvana
Hallowed be thy name
She's an Iron Maiden
She gave me a reason to fight
I guess I'm Disturbed
Before her I was a wild horse
I used to be a Rolling Stone
With you it's a beautiful day
I really do love U2...

Just a little silly poem about some musical influences on me and my writing.

Recurring nightmare

Picking this scab
The instant sting
It seems that pain
Makes my soul sing
Now as this blade
Slices a fresh wound
The symphony in my soul
Has been tuned
The claret river
Flows down my arm
My soul is dancing
To the devil's charm
It seems this time
He has finally won
After this final slice
My after life has begun
My world goes dark
I begin to cower
Standing before me
Three figures of incredible power
One dressed in devilish red
One dressed in silky white
One dressed in pure black
Each make an invite
The devil makes a pitch
Telling me my soul is tainted
I've been tormented for long
And his calling card has been painted
God's pitch is divine and pure
He speaks of salvation
An afterlife of service and atonement
For a reincarnation
Death makes the final plea
He says how he can train me
He'll mould me into death itself
A successor is who I'm meant to be
I take a second to decide
Churning over the bargains
I open my mouth to speak
"I choose" I begin…

My Heart

My heart was left on Pluto
Cold and desolate
Annexed by society
And forgotten
Cut adrift
Out of reach now
Never coming home
But I didn't planet.

My heart was warm like the Sun
A fire so hot it melted other hearts
And kept them in eternal light
Fighting away their darkness
But it has now dimmed
Since being out of orbit so long
It now only receives company
From objects passing by to other destinations.

My heart was as big as Jupiter
But now hard as Mercury
You swarmed around me
Rotating like moons
More than Saturn
Now I'm left in the ground
Trying my best to grow
I guess that's why we call it Earth...

I'm not overly sure what inspired this but I thought it was a good concept and was actually fun to write.

No words needed

No words needed
No sorry or goodbye
Take your bags from outside
And continue to cry
No longer will I be abused
No more punches and kicks
I'm numb to your games
All of your tricks

No words needed
That look is enough
You made me weak
But also tough
I say no more
You made this bed
Now lay in it
With someone else instead

No words needed
I'm finally done here
I'll no longer be a doormat
And live in fear
Because you see
We died months ago
But just because you water a plant
Doesn't mean it'll grow

No words needed
With the door shut
I can now move on
And shake this rut
No words needed
Perhaps just two
Put quite simply
Fuck you...

No words needed indeed, I could have just used the last two words to solve so
many issues.

Knock me down

Knock me down
Another right hook
My head bounces
My eyes cannot look
Kicks meet my ribs
Cracks can be heard
Hitting harder
Than any spoken word
My head is ringing
Blood flows
Who actually knew
This is how mental health goes
I stumble to my knees
Eyes bulbous and big
This next hit comes
Snapping me like a twig
But again I rise
Blood mixed with snot
And through gritted teeth I say
"Is that all you got?"

I find myself doing "rounds" with my demons and depression, sometimes i win, sometimes I'm saved by the bell and the rest of the time, well, I'm a first round casualty.
Lately I've been getting to end of the metaphorical 12 rounds and it goes to the judges, how long this will last, I don't know but what I do know is simply this, I'll keep fighting.

A milestone

Today I spoke
I don't know if people listened
I don't know if they cared
But today
I spoke
About my suicide attempt
About my depression
About how everyday is a battle
Against the things I believe are true
Today was a hard day
Today was a battle
But today, like you
I survived and kicked today's arse…

So today I spoke out in a suicide awareness course at work, the industry I work in is full of "Alpha" males who never speak about emotions, struggles and feelings. I stunned the room into silence as the speaker asked the room "Has anyone here been affected by suicide?" I raised my hand and was invited to speak about my darkest moment.
After speaking, I excused myself and sat in the toilet crying.
Never under estimate the power of speaking.

I wander

I wander
To and from places
I watch the looks
On everyone's faces
They look down at me
Judging with their looks
But aren't we told
Covers don't define books?

I wander
Roaming in isolation
Searching for sanctuary
A life without hesitation
I sit by the river
Writing in my pad
Every pivotal moment
I've ever had

I wander
This loveless land
With no-one beside me
No-one to hold my hand
All I have is a saying
That helps with this cost
Not all those who wander
Are always lost…

A few years ago my whole life turned upside down, I lost my purpose, my identity
and path.
Now I wander around trying to find all three again.
Will I find it?
Do I need to find it?
Should I find a new path to walk?
A new identity?
A new purpose?
Or ultimately is this all up to me?

Demons

I scream out loud
A monster's cry
I tilt my head back
And screech into the sky
"I've had enough
I'm not strong
I'm not meant for this world
Take me below where I belong"
A moment later
The clouds roll in
Shrouding me in shadows
"I've let my demons win"
Eerie silence follows
Broken by a thunder clap
A noise so deafening
Akin to a slap
It knocks me off my feet
I crumble to the ground
And lay in the fetal position
Without any sound
I don't know how long I laid
In that stunned state
Silently thinking
Is it too late...

This epitomises my struggles with my own depression and when I'm locked in my
maze with no escape.
I pray that you have an escape from your maze, from your demons and most of all,
an escape from your depression.

Who cares

Who cares
If all we are is a moment
A fleeting shooting star
Across the cosmos
A blink of an eye

Who cares
If we leave no mark
No greatness or success
Does that define us
Or should it?

Who cares
If one more light turns off
Snuffed out like a candle flame
A wisp of smoke remains
To show we were here at all

Who cares
Years after the event
In which we said goodbye
Who cares I ask
Well, for one, I do...

Trust me, as dark as it may seem, as isolating as it may look and as never ending
this journey may seem, people do care, not all, granted but some do.
Love your tribe, love your release and most of all, love yourself.

Break down

Break down my walls
My ivy is overgrown
Be careful of the thorns
Step into the unknown
Bring an axe and fire
Cutting through my wall
Please reach the man within
Before I fall

Break down my walls
Though they are high
I locked the door
When I said goodbye
But since then I've mellowed
I've been away too long
I no longer wish to be alone
Maybe I was wrong

Break down my walls
Save the man within
Be gentle with him
And let our love begin
I'll call you belle
You can call me beast
And together we can win
Once I've been released…

Some days I hope a saviour will ride in, shining armour and on their noble steed, slay my demons and I can live happily ever after.

Some days I feel at home isolated in my keep, looking out at the world and safe in the knowledge I am alone.

Some days I want to break down these walls I've built and let myself out into the world once more.

Some days, well, I go back to sleep…

I just want to write

I just want to write
Happy, sad or other
Yet it never turns out well
Like depression is my brother
He picks up my pen
And writes his emotions
They spew out like a river
Leaving commotions

I just want to write
About my life
What was happy
Where there was strife
Leave my pen alone
This thoughts are mine
I've been burdened
For a long time

I just want to write
About unicorns and rainbows
About perfect kisses
And where that goes
But I only spew melancholy
A wanting of sorts
A place to call home please
Away from these bad thoughts…

Can a writer ever be truly happy?
Can we ever be content?
Or are we just a mess of chaos with only a few moments of serenity?

No more

I was there
When your ego dropped
I was there
When depression topped
I was there
When you needed a friend
I was there
And didn't pretend
I was there
Being corny
I was there
When you were horny
I was there
As a plaything
I was there
And gave you a ring
I was there
To pick you off the floor
I was there
But no more…

Lately I've had to safeguard myself from people who come into my life with popcorn just to listen and then disappear and gossip.
It's a shame because I want to be open about my struggles but I found out quickly that not all who listen hear what you're saying or, quite frankly, care.

This flame

The fire inside
It used to burn bright
It burned fiercely
And always right
It's been dimmed
By life and trauma
It dipped and died
But now it burns warmer
It was rekindled
Alight again
By some people
Who thought I was just a pen
I'm so much more than a poet
I'm a man, a fighter, a bear
Never again will this light extinguish
I'm going nowhere
So come to me
And I'll help you mend
Because my flame burns for you
My tribe, my family, my friend...

I have learned that some people are meant to be in your life, others, aren't.
Blood doesn't make you immune to cutting ties, neither does length of time.
I came to realise that the smaller my circle became, the happier i became.
Perhaps ironically, I also noticed that as I cut ties, I also felt less alone, who knew
right?

Exist

I exist in a lawless state
Where no rules apply
There's no one else here
To watch me cry
No-one hears my screams
My begs and moans
My wails unanswered
No law in this land no-one owns

I exist in a forgotten land
Removed from the time line
Where every answer is a lie
Like I'm fine
People come and go
Seldom few stay
And even those give up
And leave one day

I exist in a memory
That is triggered by smell
Or the sound of a song
When things are going well
No-one remembers the days
Before I went dark
When my soul escaped
And I left my final mark…

In writing this, I was wondering about the mark I will leave on this planet or indeed, in people's lives around me.

Would it be a good thought, one tinged with sadness, or, as I also think, would I simply be forgotten all together?

I sit here

I sit here
No-one takes notice
So here I sit
A nobody to miss

I sit here
With words to speak
But no ears to listen
To even a squeak

I sit here
As an outcast
A leper or shunned
From a distant past

I sit here
People walk by
Here isolated
I start to cry

I sit here
Thoughts on my mind
There's no safety
When your head is unkind

I sit here
I need to leave
I've sat too long
Trying to breathe

I sit here
Writing away my blues
After all
What do I have to lose?

A summary of my writing process for "Almost out of the maze".
It hasn't always been pretty, yes I've cried, openly in public as well but if my tears
can save one soul, then I've won right?

Almost out of the maze

I only see you
When the moon is blue
There you appear on cue
And I can only be true

Not that I'd ever lie
Or even begin to try
Now, now wipe your eye
It's no time to cry

I sat in the rain
Suffocated by such pain
I was constantly kept under cane
And thought I was mundane

I'm better than that
I thought as I sat
My world is no longer flat
I'm no longer a doormat

I'm better now
Of that I vow
I got all the help I could allow
And wiped the dirt from my brow

I'm almost out of the maze
My head is almost cleared of haze
And even though I was knocked sideways
I can see clearer days

Even though you're no longer around
I picked myself up off the ground
My demons have no playground
And I'm firmly on the rebound...

Thank you for reading and following my journey, please take one thing from this book, you are not alone.

There are brighter days coming, I promise you that, ask for help, accept help and embrace it.

Help can come in many forms but we have to open our eyes in order to see it.
Find your tribe, find your family, find your place in this world because I know it exists.

If any of these poems resonate with you and if you so choose, feel free to follow me on instagram, my handle is Poet Dobby, drop by, say hi and know this, You're not alone.

To be continued…

Printed in Great Britain
by Amazon